DOG TRAINING 101

The Essential Guide to Raising A Happy Dog With Love. Train The Perfect Dog Through House Training, Basic Commands, Crate Training and Dog Obedience.

CESAR DUNBAR

© **Copyright 2020** by Cesar Dunbar – All rights reserved.

In no way is it legal to reproduce, duplicate, or transmit any part of this document in either electronic means or in printed format. Recording of this publication is strictly prohibited and any storage of this document is not allowed unless with written permission from the publisher.

The information provided herein is stated to be truthful and consistent, in that any liability, in terms of inattention or otherwise, by any usage or abuse of any policies, processes, or directions contained within is the solitary and utter responsibility of the recipient reader. Under no circumstances will any legal responsibility or blame be held against the author for any reparation, damages, or monetary loss due to the information herein, either directly or indirectly.

The information herein is offered for informational purposes solely, and is universal as so. The presentation of the information is without contract or any type of guarantee assurance.

Medical Disclaimer: This book does not contain any medical advice. The ideas and suggestions contained in this book are not intended as a substitute for consulting with your veterinary doctor. All matters regarding you and your dog's health require medical supervision.

Legal Disclaimer: All photos used in this book are licensed for commercial use or in the public domain.

ERRORS

Please contact us if you find any errors.

We have taken every effort to ensure the quality and correctness of this book. However, after going over the book draft time and again, we sometimes don't see the forest for the trees anymore.
If you notice any errors, we would really appreciate it if you could contact us directly before taking any other action. This allows us to quickly fix it.

Errors: errors@semsoli.com

REVIEWS

Reviews and feedback help improve this book and the author.

If you enjoy this book, we would greatly appreciate it if you were able to take a few moments to share your opinion and post a review online.

Table of Contents

INTRODUCTION……………………………………………..7

CHAPTER 1: HOW TO CHOOSE THE RIGHT DOG…………………………………………….15

CHAPTER 2: DIFFERENT DOG BREEDS EXPLAINED………………………………………......27

CHAPTER 3: HOW TO PREPARE FOR YOUR DOG'S ARRIVAL……………………………...41

CHAPTER 4: HOW TO HOUSETRAIN YOUR DOG……………………………………………..51

CHAPTER 5: CRATE TRAINING YOUR DOG………………………………………………….59

CHAPTER 6: PAPER TRAINING YOUR DOG………………………………………………….67

CHAPTER 7: HOW TO TEACH YOUR DOG BASIC OBEDIENCE SKILLS..............................73

CHAPTER 8: HOW TO TEACH YOUR DOG MORE ADVANCED SKILLS...........................87

CHAPTER 9: HOW TO TAKE CARE OF YOUR DOG...103

FINAL WORDS...113

BONUS CHAPTER: GETTING STARTED WITH PUPPY TRAINING..117

DID YOU LIKE THIS BOOK? 135

BY THE SAME AUTHOR....................................137

NOTES..142

INTRODUCTION

Did you know that dogs have 3 eyelids? That's right, 3! They have an:

- ☐ upper lid
- ☐ lower lid
- ☐ a third lid

This third eyelid protects their eyes by keeping it moist.

I'm a bit of sucker for dog facts...

When someone asks: *"Are you a dog person or a cat person?"*, I can answer it without a shadow of a doubt.

There is absolutely no hesitation when I clearly and firmly reply: *'"Dogs!"*

It's this passion for our canine friends that led me to write this book about dog training. Although I swoon over a puppy just as much as the next person, I do in fact have a **soft spot for adult dogs**. As a matter of fact, my last two rescue dogs have been adults.

Perhaps it's because I feel **they deserve a second chance** and I love being able to give them a new lease on life. After all, if you get an adult dog, it's almost certainly a rescue or one that can no longer be looked after by their owners.

There are two common reasons **why people start with a puppy**:

- **They are cute!** No one can resist a playful puppy. Also, the idea of introducing a new dog to the 'pack' (i.e. the family) at a young age is appealing as the puppy will grow with the entire unit.
- **It's believed they are easier to train.** Everyone knows that children are like sponges and absorb new information in a way that adults simply can't, so surely it's the same with dogs, right?

If you're interested in training a puppy, I wrote a bestselling book about that: **'Puppy Training 101**: *The Essential Guide to Raising a Puppy With Love. Train Your Puppy and Raise the Perfect Dog Through Potty Training, Housebreaking, Crate Training and Dog Obedience.*'

Older dogs can be trained too though, and it's really not much different. It takes a bit more effort, especially if you need to 'untrain' certain behaviors, but it's not impossible.

This book will show you how! I hope that you will be encouraged to adopt a grown-up dog, which is my ultimate aim from this book.

We have so much to learn from dogs! They:

- live in the moment
- love unconditionally
- never hold any grudges, and
- are never spiteful

Getting a dog in your home does have its set of challenges though. You will need to teach your new pet a lot of things, so that you and your dog can live in harmony. Training your dog will help in creating a rewarding relationship.

But don't worry: **you are in good hands**!

Whether you already have a dog, or are still contemplating getting one: this is the **perfect dog training guide** for you.

You will learn all the necessary information you need to choose the right dog, and turn it into a **'wooftastic', well-behaving part of the pack**: your family!

Each chapter in *'Dog Training 101'* is very practical, we're getting straight to the point.

Here are some of the things we are going to cover:

- How to choose the right dog
- Different dog breeds explained
- How to prepare for your dog's arrival
- How to housetrain your dog
- Crate training and paper training
- How to teach your dog basic obedience skills, such as 'Sit' and 'Come'
- How to teach your dog more advanced skills
- How to take care of your dog
- Bonus Chapter from my book *'Puppy Training 101'*: 'Getting Started With Puppy Training'
- And much more!

Each chapter contains lots of photos, illustrating how to teach your dog the skills you want him to learn.

You will also find a brief recap at the end of each chapter, allowing you to quickly review the **Key Takeaways**.

Finally, to keep the tone light: each chapter will start with a '**Dog Fun Fact**' and a '**Dog Joke**'. This serves as a reminder – between all the dog training info – that having a dog in our lives is so much fun!

A well-trained dog is a pleasure to have around. Let's learn how to make that happen!

CHAPTER 1: HOW TO CHOOSE THE RIGHT DOG

Dog Fun Fact: Puppies are born toothless. When they are 6–8 weeks of age, they will have developed a full set of 28 baby teeth. Shortly after, the puppy's permanent teeth will begin pushing out the milk teeth. When they are about 7 months old, a puppy will have 42 permanent teeth.

Dog Joke: Q: What do you call a dog magician? *A: A labracadabrador!*

This chapter will show you how you can choose the right dog for you. This will be the most important decision you will make when it comes to owning a dog.

Why Choose an Adult Dog?

Before we discuss breeds, let's start with the most important question: why would you choose (and train) an adult dog over a puppy?

First of all, **you give them a chance** they may not have had otherwise. Dogs are social creatures and belong in a pack. Your family could be just the pack they need!

Secondly, it's a good idea to get an older dog if you're new to the world of dogs, or aren't sure how your family and lifestyle will adapt. **Older dogs tend to be less work** (that's not to say it's all plain sailing though!) than a puppy and you can see straight away their size and temperament, so you won't get any surprises.

You can even consider a senior dog. The most neglected segment in the rescue dog world, senior dogs can be **the most rewarding companions**.

As opposed to them living out their days in a shelter or being put down, you can make the last few years of their lives extra special. They may not be as responsive as a puppy, but the saying *'you can't teach an old dog new tricks'* is simply not true!

You can, with **patience** and **persistence**.

They are a wonderful choice, if you are looking for a dog that has lower energy levels and is calm. The one thing you must be prepared for though is their shorter life span and possible expensive medical bills.

I personally have found adult dogs to be wonderful companions. If this book can inspire even just one person to adopt an older dog, then I will have done my job.

Be Honest About What You Seek and Can Give to a Dog

Once you've decided that you want a dog, next you'll ask yourself the question: *what type of dog would be the best fit for me?*

If you are clear about what you seek in a dog, and what you can offer it, it will be much easier to pick the right breed. And the lucky dog that gets to come home with you will be happy too!

Choosing the right dog is so much more than simply picking the one you find the cutest, as tempting as it may be.

One of the episodes of the National Geographic's reality TV series 'Dog Whisperer' focused entirely on so-called 'wolfdogs'. A wolfdog is a hybrid between a domesticated dog and a wolf. Wolfs have fascinated mankind for thousands of years, and some people are intrigued when they see an ad for a wolf-puppy. They'd like to own a piece of nature. And as a puppy, wolfdogs look super cute. But as they grow older, the owner quickly learns that this isn't a regular dog: wolfs are predators, and it will protect what it considers as his property at all cost. What often happens, is that – instead of recognizing that the wolfdog is simply following its nature – the owner feels his pet is misbehaving. And before you know it, the wolfdog is put in a cage, or even brought to a shelter, where it's put to sleep.

The example of wolfdogs may be a bit extreme, but I hope you see my point: if you are clear about what kind of dog would be a good match with you, you are laying the foundation for a happy union. And you'll prevent a lot of potential problems and frustrations!

So, if you are low on energy, don't get a Jack Russell: they need a lot of walking.

Do you like to go out on runs or long hikes? Then don't get a pug. Pugs have less stamina than you. Also, their body temperature rises quickly and they cannot cool themselves down.

You need to carefully assess your current situation, and figure out which dog would be a good fit, based on your lifestyle. This includes being honest with yourself about what you can really give a dog.

How To Choose The Right Dog For You

Let's start with some questions you need to ponder, and issues you need to consider:

- **Lifestyle**. What is your lifestyle like? Do you work a lot outside the house or are you at home all day? Do you travel a lot? If you do, where will you dog stay when you're not there? Do you lead an active lifestyle or more sedentary? Do you live in the city or in the country? All of these are important factors in deciding which dog is right for you.
- **Money**. Dogs are expensive. They need food, vaccinations, and can have pricey vet bills if they get sick. Calculate how much you will spend each month so you can see if your income will easily cover the expenses of having a dog.
- **Apartment or house**. This will help you determine what size dog you can manage. You should also

check to see if your apartment block will allow pets.

- **Free time**. How much time do you have spare to give your dog? Some breeds need constant attention and shouldn't be left alone.
- **Stimulation**. Some breeds are highly intelligent and active, traits that require a lot of mental stimulation and physical exercise. How much activity you can provide – both for the dog's mind and body – will help determine the breed that will be best for you.
- **Pedigree or mutt**. A pedigree has the advantage of you knowing the temperament and typical characteristics of that particular breed. A mutt can be less predictable yet adopting or buying as an adult reduces the risk of unknown traits surfacing later.
- **Grooming**. You need to consider how much time you can commit to brushing your dog's coat. Some dogs have a huge amount of fur or even dreadlocks (think the Hungarian Puli) which need extra care

and attention. Also, some breeds (such as the Bulldog) are notorious for drooling and can leave slithers of saliva here, there, and everywhere. That's not to put you off, just to warn you of the cleaning and maintenance required in taking care of a dog.

Key Takeaways

These are a few things you should really take a long, hard look at, to help you get an idea of what type of dog will be best for you. It may be your dream to have a husky, but if you live alone in a small apartment in a city and spend all day working outside of the house, it's not an ideal choice.

This chapter looked at some of the most important factors to consider when deciding on getting a dog.

There are several factors you need to consider before getting a dog. These include:

- [ ] looking at your lifestyle
- [ ] how much money you have to spend on a dog per month
- [ ] whether you live in an apartment or a house
- [ ] how much stimulation you can provide them
- [ ] how much free time you have
- [ ] how much grooming you want to do, and
- [ ] whether to get a pedigree or a mixed breed.

Once you have a clear idea of what type of dog would be a good match for you, you are one step closer to giving your future canine friend a new home.

Let's take a look at the different dog groups next, and learn their typical characteristics.

CHAPTER 2: DIFFERENT DOG BREEDS EXPLAINED

Dog Fun Fact: Dogs can dream! Don't believe me? Then go to YouTube, and search for *'These dreaming dogs make you laugh so hard'*.

Dog Joke: Q: Which dog breed is guaranteed to laugh at all of your jokes? *A: A Chi-ha-ha!*

Once you have a clear understanding of what you expect of a dog, and what you can offer it, you are ready to make an informed decision on what kind of dog breed would be a good match.

To help you decide, here are the different dog breeds divided by groups. Although all dogs have their own personalities that will determine how well they fit in your household, the dog groups generally have specific characteristics that will give you a clue what to expect.

Hound Dogs

These dogs, while they are loyal pets, are always highly stimulated by sights and smells and need to be carefully trained on 'recall'. This means if they are off the leash and you call their name, they come back to you rather than galloping off into the distance chasing something.

Hounds make wonderful pets; but they need plenty of exercise, otherwise they can get bored and start chewing on things. Breeds in this group include Beagles,

Greyhounds, Whippets, Ridgebacks, Salukis, and Bloodhounds.

Sporting Dogs

One of the friendliest of the dog groups, the sporting dogs include breeds such as Receivers, Springer Spaniels, Labradors, Pointers, and Setters.

While being responsive to training and great with people, they have a huge amount of energy and need to be exercised regularly and kept mentally stimulated with training and games.

Working Dogs

The dogs in this group were originally bred for working purpose such as guarding or hunting. Breeds include Huskies, Akitas, Dobermans, and Great Danes.

They are fiercely loyal and can be easily trained; providing you manage to establish yourself as the alpha in the 'pack'; otherwise, they can be tricky to handle.

This group is best for people who have past experience with dogs.

Herding Dogs

Herding dogs – such as Collies, German Shepherds, and Corgis – make exciting and loyal pets yet they are hard work and demanding. Apartment living is not suitable for them and they need lots of exercise and space to run around.

They are also very intelligent; which, while being great for training, is a problem if you are not prepared to give them the mental stimulation they need.

Terriers

Terriers can make loyal companions and are great for those that live in smaller houses or apartments. Given their size, they need less exercise than say the herding or working dogs, but they still need regular walks and games, albeit on a smaller scale.

West Highland White Terriers, Jack Russells, Staffordshire Bull Terriers, and Norwich Terriers are all popular breeds.

Non-Sporting Group

This includes a huge mix of breeds such as Dalmatians, Chow Chows, Bichon Frise, French Bulldog, Poodles, and

Finnish Spitz. Each breed needs to be carefully assessed before getting it, as each one is uniquely different from the other.

Bichon Frises and Bulldogs, for example, are great apartment dogs, but need careful training as they can be quite stubborn. Dalmatians are entertaining breeds and can be trained easily, but need plenty of exercise and games to keep them happy. You need to make sure you have the time and energy to give them the stimulation they need.

A tragic example of what can happen if you don't, is the aftermath of the animated Disney classic '101 Dalmatians', which was released in 1996. In the movie, Dalmatians are cute and fun. After the movie hit the box office, demand for Dalmatian puppies boomed. However, in real life Dalmatians can be a handful. Not everyone has what it takes to give them the attention and care they need. What happened? According to a 1997 New York

Times Article, animal shelters reported a sharp increase in the number of unwanted Dalmatian dogs they received.

I've said it before, but I will stress it again: if you want to live happily ever after with your dog:

- know what you want, and
- know what you can give.

Toy group

These pint-sized canines are a good choice for those that live in an apartment. While they still need some exercise, they are mostly happy relaxing at home and don't need a vast amount of space to be content.

Despite their small size, they are often one of the bravest dogs in the park. They don't let their tiny stature hold them back! Some toy breeds are easier to train than others, so research the type you want thoroughly.

Toy breeds include the Bolognese, Chihuahuas, Pugs, and the Chinese Crested Dog.

Mutts

Mutts or mixed-breed dogs shouldn't be underestimated as they can make the most loving companions and also come with a couple of distinct advantages. They can take the best qualities out of their purebred parents or past relatives, which can give them great personalities and characteristics. Moreover, their mixed gene pool makes them less prone to illnesses that are common in specific pure breeds.

If you get one as an adult, ask the person you are getting it from if you can spend a bit of time with it, before you commit to adopting it, as this will be a great indication of how it behaves. It will also be a good opportunity for you to see how the dog will fit with your lifestyle.

Knowing what you can truly give to a dog is the first step in choosing the best breed for you. The next is matching your lifestyle to the most appropriate dog. Finally, you can actually start searching for the dog you want and eventually take one home with you.

Key Takeaways

In this chapter, we looked at the different dog groups and their typical characteristics. Use this to decide which breed is best for you.

Once you have a better understanding of your lifestyle, you will be ready to accept a dog into your life. There are several groups of dogs to choose from:

- Hound Dogs

- Sporting Dogs
- Working Dogs
- Herding Dogs
- Terriers
- Non-Sporting Dogs
- Toys, and last but certainly not least,
- Mutts or Mixed Breeds.

In the next chapter, we will take look at what you need to do to prepare for the arrival of your new, four-legged friend!

CHAPTER 3: HOW TO PREPARE FOR YOUR DOG'S ARRIVAL

Dog Fun Fact: At the end of the song *'A Day in the Life'*, The Beatles recorded a high-pitched whistle that only dogs can hear! Paul McCartney did this specially for his dog, Martha.

Dog Joke: Q: What do you get when you cross a dog and a calculator? *A: A friend you can count on!*

Bringing a dog home with you is an important step. More than likely, your new dog will be nervous or overly excited, so his senses will be on high alert.

To make sure the arrival of your pet goes as smoothly as possible and he feels welcome to your home, here are a few key tips to help you.

Make Sure Your Family Is Prepared

First of all, it's essential everyone in your household knows that the dog is arriving that day, so they can be prepared for his arrival. This will involve making sure everything is tidied away (just in case your favorite shoes become a potential object to chew) and breakable items are put out of harm's way (wagging tails on excited dogs don't bode well for delicate ornaments). Also, make sure that everyone knows exactly what their responsibilities are beforehand, such as feeding him, taking him out for walks, and grooming him. This will help make the transition of your pet's arrival that little bit easier and quicker to establish a stable routine.

Buy All The Dog Items Beforehand

Before the dog actually arrives, make sure you go out and buy all the things you need. This includes a:

- [ ] his collar
- [ ] a leash
- [ ] a water bowl
- [ ] a food bowl
- [ ] toys
- [ ] a bed
- [ ] a grooming brush, and
- [ ] plenty of dog food.

Introducing a new brand of dog food at this time can be a difficult change for your dog's stomach to handle and, coupled with the excitement and anxiety, could make him feel sick. Ask the previous owner what your dog was eating before and buy the same brand in the beginning, to avoid too many changes in one go. Once your dog has settled in, you can gradually begin to introduce a different type of food if you want.

Find a Vet

Next, get the contact of your nearest vet, so you know who to call in case of an emergency and who to go to for annual check-ups. This is also a good moment to try and find out the health history of your dog, such as any underlying conditions you should be aware of and when the last flea and worm treatment was. When your dog finally arrives, it's a good idea to take him to the vet to microchip him or, if he already has a microchip, to update the information with your details.

Take A Couple of Days Off

The day you bring your dog to your home is important. Ideally, try bringing him home on a day when you have a couple of days ahead free – such as on a Friday evening if you don't work weekends – so you can be around to reassure him and help him to adapt to the new home and your family. Let him free to explore the entire house and sniff every corner; he will want to familiarize himself with his new environment.

He's Here! Show Your Dog Around

As soon as your dog arrives, show him where his toilet place is, whether that's your garden or a patch of grass outside of your apartment. Give him time to use the area and when he goes, praise him a lot to reinforce that this is the standard place to do his business.

Dogs and Children

If you have children, it's important you introduce them to the dog slowly and gradually. When you first visit the dog – be it at a shelter or with a previous owner – you should ask how he is around children. If he is (apparently) fine, introduce your children and the dog to each other in the environment he is most comfortable in. From these initial reactions, you will have a good understanding of how he and your children will get on.

Once you bring the dog home, you are placing him in unfamiliar territory. Having lots of attention may be a bit overwhelming for him, especially as children tend to get very hands-on with dogs. Make sure they get to know each other slowly; the fun part of playing with the dog will come soon enough.

When to Start Dog Training

Your dog's training should start in the first week of his arrival. Start small, rather than launching into a complex training program. The first week should be about observing your dog's habits and any tendencies that he may have.

For example, when a friend of mine, Julie King, adopted her mixed breed dog (which seemed to have a bit of almost every breed imaginable!), she found that Lola, her dog, had a habit of picking up loose bits of paper – be it from a notebook, a toilet roll, or a newspaper – and then happily rip them apart into tiny shreds that would get everywhere. *"I kept an eye on Lola for the first few days and whenever I saw her reaching to get some paper, I would reprimand her"*, said Julie, who also searched for ways to keep paper out of sight and reach from Lola. *"Whenever a newspaper for example was left on the table and Lola didn't touch it, I would also make sure she was rewarded for that with a massive fuss or a little doggie treat. In the end, it worked and she lost interest in paper and just started chewing apart her toys instead."* Keep an eye on undesirable habits such as this and teach your dog from the very beginning that behavior like that isn't acceptable in his new pack.

Put all these tips into practice for your dog's arrival and things should go smoothly. After he has settled in, the time is right for play, to integrate him into your family, and to start thinking about more advanced training.

Key Takeaways

In this chapter, you learned how to prepare for your dog's arrival, and how to welcome him into your home.

- Make sure you have bought all the things your dog will need (such as food, food bowls, toys, and a leash) and that everyone in the household knows their responsibilities for taking care of the dog.
- When your dog arrives, give them plenty of time and space to explore their new environment. Show them the toilet area and praise them when they use it correctly. Make sure you bring your dog home on a day when you have a couple of days free after, so you can be with your dog in the early stages.
- Introduce your dog to your children slowly, so they can both get used to each other. Keep an eye out for

any undesirable habits and tendencies that the dog may have, in order to nip the issue in the bud from the very beginning.

Yay, your dog is finally home!

Next, let's learn how you can use housetraining to turn the new member of the pack into a well-behaving, obedient dog.

CHAPTER 4: HOW TO HOUSETRAIN YOUR DOG

Dog Fun Fact: President Lyndon Johnson had 2 beagles. Their names? 'Him' and 'Her'!

Dog Joke: Q: How are a dog and a marine biologist alike? *A: One wags a tail and the other tags a whale.*

One of the most important things your dog can learn are basic housetraining skills. As an adult dog, he may already have been taught this, yet if he has been a rescue dog for a large chunk of his life, there is a chance that he may not be housetrained. This chapter will show you the best way to housetrain your dog.

Important: Stick to a Disciplined Routine

It's a common misconception that adult dogs are harder to housetrain than puppies: that's not the case at all! In fact, housetraining adult dogs is usually much easier and doesn't take that long. If you stick with a disciplined routine, and commit to your training, you can housetrain a dog in a week or less.

Now, let's learn some steps and tips to housetrain your new adult canine friend!

Begin Housetraining on Day 1

Make sure housetraining begins from day one. It's easier if you start housetraining as soon as your dog arrives, so he knows where the designated toilet area is in his new environment. It's a good idea to take a few days off work in the first week. Being on hand to observe and help your dog understand where he has to go will help quicken the pace of housetraining. If you can't take time off work, see if another family or house member is around to housetrain in the first few days, or hire a dog walker or trainer to do the housetraining for you.

Keep Feeding Times Consistent

It is important to feed your dog on consistent times, so that bathroom breaks become regular too. Feed your dog at specific times. Once he has finished eating, take his bowl away, so the feeding time and toilet time become a regular habit.

Keep Toilet Times Consistent Too

Dogs will go to the toilet about four times a day. Keep these times consistent, so it becomes a part of the routine. Take your dog to the designated toilet area and give him time to go. It helps to keep this area the same every time as the dog will recognize it and associate it with toilet time.

Reward Your Dog For Doing His Business Outside

When you take your dog to the designated toilet area and he successfully does his business there, make sure you reward him with plenty of fuss. A scratch on the head with an encouraging 'good boy' or 'good girl' is enough positive reinforcement.

How to Act if Your Dog Pees Inside The House

What should you do if you catch them in the act of going to the toilet in your house? You should startle them by clapping your hands or slapping a magazine on a hard surface. This will be enough to make them stop, and for you to quickly whisk them outside to finish doing their business. Once they've gone outside, give them plenty of praise.

This method is preferable over shouting at your dog, which will simply make them scared of you. Also, you should only use the startle method when you actually catch your dog in the act of doing its business in your house. If you do it afterwards, the dog won't understand and no matter how many times you point at the mess on the floor, he simply can't make the connection between his misbehavior, the mess, and your anger.

Notice The Dog's Signals

Pay close attention to your dog and his signals that he needs to go. Some are very obvious. For example, they will do things such as waiting by the door when they need to go. Others don't give any indication and simply go. You have to keep a very close eye to any clues they give and take them outside straight away to go to the toilet.

Be Kind, Not Harsh

If your dog doesn't make it in time, don't be harsh on him. He probably simply doesn't understand yet that the outside is for the toilet and the inside isn't.

However, if he does go inside, make sure you clean the area thoroughly. Obviously, this is good for your home to keep it clean but also, if your dog smells his own scent in the same spot where he went before, he will be more likely to go there again.

Key Takeaways

This chapter showed you one of the most important skills your dog needs to learn: housetraining.

- Prepare the house and family for the arrival of the new pack member.
- It's best to take a few days off work when your dog arrives (if you can) so you can really help his progress with housetraining. This training should

start immediately to avoid any bad habits developing.

- Having a regular feeding and watering time will really help regulate his toilet time which, in turn, will help you better predict when your dog will need to go. If he does go inside, stay calm and be kind. He will learn soon enough!

Unfortunately, not all dogs are totally responsive, and some may be harder to train than others. If you've tried all the steps outlined above, yet your dog is still not fully housetrained after a week, then you may want to think about using a technique known as crate training. We'll discuss that next.

CHAPTER 5: CRATE TRAINING YOUR DOG

Dog Fun Fact: The largest dog breed is the Irish Wolfhound. The largest dog ever recorded was Zeus, a Great Dane, who measured a whopping 44 inches tall in 2011!

Dog Joke: Q: What kind of dog chases anything red? *A: A Bulldog!*

If you are unsuccessful in housetraining your dog, I recommend you try a different method: crate training.

What is Crate Training?

Crate training is when you leave your dog inside the crate a bit before it's toilet time, and release him when he needs to go.

Once he has been, you praise him, let him roam around the house for a while and put him back in the cage again, before its time for the next toilet round. The dog will still eat and drink outside of the cage as usual. As dogs never spoil the area they sleep in, they will wait until you let them out before eliminating their waste and so, the association between being outside and doing their toilet business is fixed.

If you feel this sounds like a mean technique, it is generally perceived in the dog world as not being a cruel practice. Firstly, dogs tend to like being in their dens, as it makes them feel secure. Secondly, it only takes a few days for this training to work (many owners say it takes just three days) so they will be housetrained much quicker. Finally, once they understand where their designated toilet area is, you can let them out of the crate to roam freely around the house.

Crate Training: Things to Consider

If you decide crate training is the route you want to go down, here are some important things to consider and do:

- ☐ Don't let your dog have access to food and water all throughout the day. Instead, make sure their feeding and watering times are set at specific times. This helps to regulate your dog's bowel and bladder movements, so he goes at more regular times. Otherwise, he will eat and drink throughout the day and find it harder to control when he needs to go.

- The crate has to be a good size for you dog. They should have enough room to be able to stand up, stretch out, and turn around comfortably without being cramped. However, it shouldn't be too big that they have ample room to walk around, otherwise they will use one side to sleep on and the other side as a toilet area, which will completely defeat the purpose of this method.
- One of the most important things about the crate is that it should never be used to punish your dog. You are simply using it now as a housetraining tool. After housetraining, you can leave the crate open, so your dog has his own little den while still being able to roam around the house. Make sure you leave the crate in the busiest part of your house, such as your living room or kitchen, so your dog, even being inside the crate, will feel a part of the family. Leaving him by himself will just make him feel isolated and sad.
- When it is time to let your dog out of the crate, make sure the minute you open it, you lead him

straight to his bathroom spot. It's a good idea that he knows the area before using the crate technique. This way, he already has some memory that this was the spot where he went before.

How to Crate Train a Dog

Keeping the above tips in mind, here's how to put crating into practice:

- Having a set feeding time is important as you will quickly get into the routine of knowing when your dog will need to go. This is vital for the next step.
- About 20 minutes before their usual regular toilet time, put the dog in the crate. This leeway in time acts as a buffer to protect your home from any accidental toilet moments inside the house.
- When their scheduled time to use the toilet comes, take them out of the crate and straight to the designated toilet spot.
- If they go, give them a bunch of praise and let them wander freely around the house. Only put them

back in the crate when it's 20 minutes before the next scheduled time.

- If they don't go, put them back in the crate and wait another 10 minutes. Then, release them and take them back to the toilet spot. Wait a few minutes to give them the chance to go. If they don't go again, then repeat this step until they finally relieve themselves.
- Never make your dog wait too long in the above step. If they are really desperate, they will just simply go in the crate and this can be detrimental to your training. If your dog is very small, reduce the 10 minutes to 5 minutes.
- If your dog is sick and has diarrhea, crate training is not ideal. They can't control their need to go and will end up having to go in their crate. This not only sets your training back, it also puts the dog in a highly uncomfortable situation.

Key Takeaways

Crate training involves using a crate to teach your dog to associate the outdoors with toilet time. It's a highly effective way of housetraining and many dog owners use this method.

Don't have a lot of time? Then paper training might be a better suitable method. We'll discuss that in the next chapter.

CHAPTER 6: PAPER TRAINING YOUR DOG

Dog Fun Fact: A dog's nose is so powerful that they can smell it if someone is sick. According to scientific research, dogs can discover lung cancer by sniffing a person's breath. And some dogs' noses are so well developed that they can even detect cancer that is still too small to be detected by a doctor! So, make sure you pay attention when a dog acts funny around you.

Dog Joke: Q: What is a dog's favorite instrument? *A: A trombone!*

While the crate method is highly effective, it's not practical for those that work full-time. It's unfair to leave your dog in the crate too long. He probably won't be able to hold it, so he will end up going inside the cage. In this case, you may be better off using the paper training method.

What is Paper Training?

Paper training is a method where you lay down old newspapers, to signal where your dog needs to go. Nowadays, there are also 'dog pads' which are similar to fake grass or toilet mats. They simply look nicer than newspapers and are easy to wash and reuse.

The paper method is ideal for those that don't have an outdoor area for their dog to relieve himself. Just bear in mind: once you've trained your dog to use the paper method inside, it will be hard to retrain them to go outside in the future. However, you can use the paper method in the beginning inside and gradually move it closer to the outside, before fully committing to leaving it outdoors.

How to Paper Train a Dog

To housetrain your dog using the paper method: begin by laying down some old newspaper (or your dog pad or toilet mat, if you have one) and encourage your dog to do his business there. Make sure you cover a large area with paper, to give him plenty of space. Leave it far away from his food and water.

Every time he goes on the paper, make sure you praise him with a scratch to the head, some kind-sounding words, or even a little biscuit.

The paper will obviously get dirty quite quickly, so keep it clean by removing the old paper and adding new pieces. If you let it get too dirty, your dog won't want to use it and will find another part of your house to go in. When you do take away the old paper, leave one piece that is a little bit dirty so your dog can smell his own scent and recognize it as his place to go.

Gradually, as your dog gets used to his toilet spot, you can reduce the size by laying down less and less sheets of paper until it's just a few sheets big. This is the moment you can also begin to move it to the spot you want, whether that's in a different room or outside.

Key Takeaways

Paper training is an alternative to crate training. This is a better option if you work full time, or live in a place without an outdoor area. With paper training, your dog will be trained to go inside, but in a designated spot. However, the paper method can still be used if your plan is to get your dog to go outside. You just need to gradually move the paper toilet area to where you want your dog to do his business.

In the next chapter, we will look at basic obedience training for your dog. This is critical to teach him fundamental skills that will:

- help him integrate better into your family, and

☐ make sure he remains well-behaved.

CHAPTER 7: HOW TO TEACH YOUR DOG BASIC OBEDIENCE SKILLS

Dog Fun Fact: The first modern guide dogs were trained to help soldiers who had lost their sight due to exposure to mustard gas in WWI.

Dog Joke: Q: Where do dogs go after their tails fall off?

A: *The re-tail store!*

This chapter will look at what obedience training your dog needs to have, the basic skills to be a well-behaved dog.

Teaching your dog the basic commands will help manage any behavioral problems your dog may have. It is possible to go to training classes, yet this requires commitment, time, and money on your part. When it comes to fundamental obedience, you can do this yourself. This is not only good fun, but will really help build a bond between you and your dog!

There are five basic skills that you can teach your dog in a matter of days:

- ☐ Sit
- ☐ Come
- ☐ Down
- ☐ Stay

☐ Leave It

Let's take a look at how you train your dog with these commands!

Teaching the Command 'Sit'

This is such a useful command, especially in situations such as waiting to cross the road or at meal times. It's also one of the easiest to teach.

First, begin by holding a treat near to your dog's nose while making sure it's concealed enough, so your dog can smell it but can't lunge forward and snatch it. Raise your hand so that his head will follow the hand with the treat in it. This will naturally make his back and bottom lower in the sit position. As soon as he is sat down, say clearly 'Sit' before giving him the treat and some praise.

Some dogs pick this up quicker than others. For example, a border collie will usually learn this very quickly, whereas a Chihuahua may need a little more time. However, if you repeat these steps several times, eventually your dog will get it. Use this command to help keep your dog calm and under control in times when he could get overexcited.

Teaching the Command 'Come'

The 'Come' command is especially useful for teaching hound dogs who, once they've caught the scent or sight of something, have a hard time forgetting about it and will go after it, no matter how much you are yelling for them to come back. It's not because they mean to be disobedient; they simply are wired this way. However, teaching them 'Come' can be enough to condition them to come back to you, even if that scent is just irresistible. It's not just hound dogs though; all dogs should learn this basic command, to avoid problems if your dog makes a bolt through an open door, or manages to get free from his leash.

To teach 'Come', secure your dog with his collar and his lead. Put a bit of space between you by asking him to 'Sit' and then move away from him to the length of the leash.

Crouch down and say 'Come', while giving a tug on the leash. There is a good chance that simply seeing you crouching down will be enough for them to come running over before you even need to tug on the leash. Once he comes over and is next to you, give him a treat and an affectionate rub.

Keep practicing these steps until your dog comes on command. Once you feel comfortable, then try without the leash yet choose your spot carefully; a bus park with children playing and other dogs roaming around may be too stimulating for your dog to ignore. Do it in a quiet, safe place, before moving to busier areas.

Teaching the Command 'Down'

Find a quiet, safe spot to practice the 'Down' command – your home is perfect – as it can be a tricky command for some dogs to learn. Especially those that are naturally quite anxious. The 'Down' position is submissive, which can put dogs at some level of unease. However, some dogs – such as Labradors – generally learn this pretty quickly and are happy to adopt this posture at your command.

To teach the 'Down' position, put a treat in your hand and hold it in front of your dog's nose. Once he knows what's in your hand, lower your hand slowly to the floor, letting him follow your movements with his head. You then need to move your hand along the ground which should help his body follow his head. Say 'Down' as he adopts the down position and then give him the treat.

Try this every day until he gets it. You dog may try to take some steps forward or sit up. If he does, simply say 'no' and move your hand out of sight before repeating the steps again. It may be tempting, but it's best not to push him into the down position, as this will simply take the strain off him and he won't learn how to do it himself. This may take a bit of time; but stay patient, keep trying, and eventually he will get it.

Teaching the Command 'Stay'

The 'Stay' command is an essential one for your dog to learn. Keep in mind though that he can only move onto 'Stay' training once he really understands the 'Sit' command, and can perform it well.

To teach him to stay, begin by instructing your dog to sit. Once he has sat down, hold your hand towards him like the 'Stop' sign and clearly say 'Stay'. Slowly take a couple of steps back and, if he stays put, give him a treat. Continue the training, but increase your steps each time.

Be careful to only reward your dog when he stays put and not when he comes bounding over. If he comes running over after you have said 'good boy', that's ok. But if he runs to you and then you praise him, he may begin to think that 'Stay' means something else. In the beginning of the training, keep your dog in the sit and stay position for a short time – even a couple of seconds – and build it up from there. Don't forget to always reward him for when he stays!

The 'Stay' command can be a tricky to teach, so be patient and you will get there in the end. Some dogs – such as Bulldogs – may find the stay position quite easy as they tend to be low-energy dogs. However, dogs with higher levels of energy or working dogs may find the 'Stay' command a challenge and need a bit more time, no matter how much they want to please you.

Teaching the Command 'Leave It'

After teaching your dog the other four commands, you can now move onto the 'Leave It' command. This command can be very useful for when your dog picks up something undesirable or dangerous in his mouth, or just so happens to be edging towards picking up your food. To teach your dog 'Leave It', you have to follow two steps.

The first requires you to hold a small treat in both hands, before presenting one of your hands to your dog and firmly saying, 'Leave It'. Allow your dog to sniff your hand (some dogs may try and paw at your hand or even start barking) but make sure you ignore him. Let him continue until he finally stops and moves away from your hand. At that point, you can give him the treat from the other hand.

Keep repeating this action. The aim is for your dog to automatically back off from the first hand the moment you say, 'Leave It'. Once he has that mastered, keep practicing, only giving a reward when he backs away from your first hand, looks up at you and makes eye contact.

That's step one. If your dog is managing that, he is ready to move onto step two which is a bit more challenging.

Start by putting a treat on the floor in front of your dog and hide it using your hand. Your dog will probably begin by staring intently at this treat, but eventually he will look up at you. When he does, reward him with another treat that you have in your hand. Try this a few times, until he's really got it.

Next, you can move onto the even more challenging part. Put the treat on the floor but just hover your hand over the treat so your dog can still see it. As he gets better and more used to this, keep your hand higher above the treat. Remember to repeat 'Leave It' every time you do this.

Once he has really got the hang of that, you can try doing it while standing up; just have your foot ready to quickly cover the treat if he lunges forward to get it.

This is the hardest of all of these five commands to teach, as it is pure instinct for your dog to snatch up the food while it's there. For this reason, take this training slow and steady – it may take some time and that's ok. If you find you have advanced too quickly and now he has problems, just go back to the earlier stages and build up confidence.

Key Takeaways

This chapter looked at how to teach your dog the five basic commands that will be an excellent start to having a well-behaved and obedient dog.

Remember, every dog has their own pace and some may need a bit more patience and effort than others. However, these obedience skills are easy to teach, and in time, your dog will master them.

- ☐ The five basic commands are sit, come, down, stay, and leave it.
- ☐ To teach these, you need patience, effort, time, persistence, and treats that your dog loves.

Now that we have the basic commands down to a tee, we can move onto more advanced training for your dog, which we will look at in the next chapter.

CHAPTER 8: HOW TO TEACH YOUR DOG MORE ADVANCED SKILLS

Dog Fun Fact: Just like every human has a unique fingerprint, every dog has a unique nose print. One problem though: because their noses are always wet, taking nose prints will be really hard!

Dog Joke: Q: What do you call a large dog that meditates? *A: Aware wolf!*

Now that your dog knows the basic commands, you can move onto more advanced training. If you plan to do agility or sports with your dog, you will need specific commands that will take time to teach and practice. These training tips are great if you just want to have fun with your dog and see what he can do. They will also make a solid foundation of training if you decide you want to compete with your dog in the future.

Teaching Your Dog How to Fetch

Fetch is such a classic game to play with your dog that it can be surprising when your dog doesn't want to play it or just simply doesn't understand it. To some dogs – especially sporting dogs or hounds – fetch comes a little more naturally and can be easy to teach. To others, such as toy dogs, fetch seems an alien concept. However, it *can* be taught. Once your dog gets the hang of it, they usually love playing fetch for hours.

Here are some tips to teach your dog how to fetch:

- You may need to begin from square one by teaching your dog how to chase an object. First, start by waving the object in front of him, until he reaches up to grab it. Once he snatches it in his mouth, reward him. Repeat this several times, until he associates picking up that object in his mouth with a treat. Next, throw the object just a short distance away. After teaching him the association between the object and the treat, he should run after it. When he does, make sure you reward him when he picks the object up. Keep practicing like this, until he has the hang of chasing it. Don't rush this step; take your time getting it right and really helping your dog understand the 'chase' idea.

- The next step is to get your dog to bring the object (be it a toy or a stick) back to you. You can try using the 'Come' command to draw him back. If that doesn't work, and he is standing far away from you with the object in his mouth while staring blankly at you, show him another toy and encourage him back to you by waving it in front of you or throwing it a very short distance behind you. This will help him get used to the idea of coming back to you after you have thrown an object for him to chase. Keep practicing, until he starts coming back with the first object and praise him when he does.

- To teach him to drop the object, say 'Drop' and show him the second object. If he drops the first object to get the second, reward him. Keep practicing until he is able to drop the object just from hearing 'Drop', and without seeing the second object.

- Some dogs will bound off into the distance once they've caught the object, and it can be difficult to get them back. If that sounds like your dog, then try teaching 'fetch' on a leash. You may want to use a lengthy leash for this exercise. Throw the object no more than the length of the leash and let your dog chase it. Once he catches it, tug gently on the leash to encourage him to come back. Once he returns back to you, reward him. Keep practicing these steps until he understands that, after chasing, he should come back to you. It takes time, but within a couple of weeks or so, he will start getting the hang of it.
- Sometimes, the issue is that the dog will come back but drop the object along the way. If this happens, say 'bring it back' and encourage him to go and pick up the object again. This may take some patience, but once he does it once, be sure to give

your dog plenty of praise and a reward to encourage him to do it again.

- Finally, make sure that you are using a toy or something your dog really likes. If he never shows any interest in sticks for example, trying to teach him to chase one will be hard, as he simply won't want to go and get it. Using his favorite toy is a good place to start.

Teaching the Command 'Place'

This is a handy skill for your dog to know, as it will teach him to go to a particular place and wait there. This can be useful if guests come to your house, and your dog gets over-excited when they arrive. You can say 'Place', which will command him to go to the designated spot and wait there, which should calm him. Before learning this skill, your dog should be very responsive to the 'Sit' and 'Stay' commands.

You can teach the 'Place' command by putting the leash on your dog and saying the word 'Place' or whatever word you prefer, such as 'Bed' or 'Home'. As you say the word, lead your dog to the spot you are teaching him to go to. Once he is there, give him a treat. Keep practicing with the leash several times, before you try without the leash. If he can't quite master it off the leash, that's fine; just try again with the leash on, until he knows exactly what you are asking of him.

Once he fully understands and can go to his place when you ask, you can then command him to sit, or lie down and stay. Make sure he stays down for about 10 seconds, before giving him a treat. Keep practicing until he can stay in his place for about two or three minutes.

Asking to Go Outside

You may have established your dog's toilet routine. However, sometimes even the tightest schedule can change and your dog may need to go at a different time to normal. In this case, wouldn't it be handy if your dog could tell you that he wants to go?

It is possible to teach him how to show he wants to go outside for the toilet.

Here are the steps how:

- Start by hanging something that makes a noise near to the door which you use to go out with your dog for the toilet. Make sure it is well-secured and is low enough for your dog to reach it.

- A good example is a toy with some little bells on it. It's best not to hang it on the door itself. Otherwise it will ring every time you go out, which will send out mixed signals to your dog.
- Once you've done that, get into the habit of ringing the bells every time you go out with your dog for the toilet, to help associate toilet breaks with the ringing of the bells.
- Before you go out, if your dog sniffs the bells or touches them, reward him, so he can make that link between interacting with the bells, the sound, and doing his business.
- Keep rewarding this behavior, until he is able to touch the bells himself every time he goes out to the toilet. If he needs to go, he will be able to alert you by touching the bells.

Teaching the Command 'Heel'

Teaching your dog to heel means that he walks next to you by your leg as you walk. It's good to keep your dog under control and calm. It's also an important skill if you plan to do agility tests or competitions with your dog. To teach 'Heel', stand still with your dog next to you. He should be right by your leg and looking in the same direction as you. Say firmly: 'Heel', and take a couple of steps forward. Ideally your dog will follow you and stay next to your leg. If he does that, give him a reward and build up the distance that you walk.

Teaching 'Heel' is not always that easy. It may be necessary to have a training collar or leash that will help speed up the learning and show your dog exactly what you expect of them. Do some research into which training collars are best for your dog. Alternatively, you can try using a heel stick, which you use to gently tap your dog on his leg that is on the other side of you, to encourage him to move into position and walk next to you.

Whenever your dog successfully walks to heel, make sure you give him a treat to reward his good behavior.

How to Get Your Dog to Stop Barking

Barking is a natural form of communication for a dog and can be extremely useful to alert of danger or intruders. However, sometimes barking goes beyond that and can be the result of poor habits and the dog being unintentionally conditioned to bark. Although this is annoying, it means it can be trained out of him with a lot of patience and understanding.

The first thing to remember is not to shout at him. He may interpret that as you joining in and that can make him even more excited and bark even more. Likewise, don't try to stop him with a gentle, soothing voice. That can be understood as you giving a positive signal which will make him bark more.

There are a few different ways to teach your dog not to bark. You can try using a head halter, which gently forces the mouth closed when he barks without any reason. It's not a cruel method and it doesn't hurt him. It is a quick way of managing unwanted barking. Reward him with praise when he stops barking. Another way to stop him barking is to create distractions to keep his mind off whatever it is that is making him bark. A sharp slap of a magazine on the table will be enough to startle him. When he stops, you can reward him.

My friend Sam Parker had a Jack Russell cross that was practically perfect in every way; except when it came to barking. *"Bruce would just bark at everything. The postman, the neighbor's cat, the wind. Everything"*, said Sam told me. *"Shouting at him encouraged him more so I left a rolled-up magazine by the table and every time he barked for nothing, I would hit the table. It would startle him enough to stop and then I would reward him. It took a while and he is still pretty vocal but he's much better now, and calmer."*

Other Dog Tricks

Teaching your dog tricks is not only something to show off to your friends or guests, it's actually a great way to bond with your dog and have fun with him. Here are some additional tricks you can teach him:

- **Bark on Command**. You need to encourage your dog to bark while saying 'Speak' or 'Bark', and reward him when he does.
- **Shake the Paw**. This is actually one of the easiest tricks to teach, especially if you have a treat in your hand. Your dog will naturally give you their paw if they can't get the treat with their mouths. Try to make it happen so that they give you their paw at

the same time as you say 'Give me Your Paw', or simply 'Paw'. When this happens, reward them.

- **Roll Over**. Make sure your dog responds to 'Down' first. Then use the command 'Roll', as you simultaneously encourage him to roll over with a treat.

Key Takeaways

In this chapter, we looked at some of the more advanced commands you can teach your dog. These give you an idea of what your dog can do as well as using training to treat undesirable behavior. If you decide to do competitions with your dog, you will need to teach him even more advanced skills, which can be so much fun for both you and your canine friend.

- The advanced commands we covered here are fetch, place, ask to go outside, heel, and to stop barking.
- Advanced commands are more challenging and should only be practiced once your dog has totally mastered the basic skills. You will also need plenty of patience. However, the results will be rewarding!

In the next chapter, we will look at how to take proper care for your dog.

CHAPTER 9: HOW TO TAKE CARE OF YOUR DOG

Dog Fun Fact: Josh Hutcherson, who played Peeta in 'The Hunger Games' film series, adopted a Pit Bull that had been at the Downey Animal shelter for 110 days. The dog arrived at the shelter with a broken leg and two missing toes. However, he was able to get surgery before

Hutcherson took him home. He named him Driver, after Ryan Gosling's character in the 2011 movie Drive.

Dog Joke: Q: What's a dog's favorite dessert? *A: Pupcakes!*

In this chapter, you will learn some of the most important things to consider when taking care of your dog. This will include proper hygiene, exercising your dog, and traveling.

Visit The Vet

When you first get your dog and he is settled into your home, take him for an overall check-up at the vets. This will detect any underlying medical conditions that perhaps you weren't aware of, and reassure you that he is in good health.

If he is overdue on his flea and worm treatment, make sure you get that done too, to prevent him getting them. Once fleas are in the household, it can be a nightmare getting rid of them. Your dog should have annual vet check-ups to make sure he is healthy.

If your dog has long fur, make sure he is groomed often, whether you decide to do it yourself, or take him to a professional groomer. This is more than aesthetics; regular grooming can help prevent skin irritations too.

Once you know he is healthy and been given the all-clear by the vet, here are some other things to think about.

The Best Nutrition

Your dog, like a human, needs a healthy, balanced diet. Get the best quality food that you can afford, to ensure your dog is kept in good shape and gets all the nutrients that he needs. You can choose between dry or wet food, and each one comes with its own advantages. While dry food is great for the dog's teeth, wet food can build up plaque. However, dogs tend to prefer wet food. So, a good option is to provide a mix of both dry and wet feed and brush your dog's teeth regularly. Some dog owners opt for the raw food diet which can be good for your dog. However, if you decide to do that, make sure you do your research and consult your vet first.

How often (and how much) you feed your dog depends on its size and how much it exercises. Follow the manufacturer guidelines on the dog food packets to get a good idea of how much food your dog needs. Make sure you feed your dog at regular times, to help with his housetraining and to build a comforting routine for him.

How to Make Your Dog a Part of The Family

Remember, dogs are social creatures and see you as their pack. As a result, they want to be close to you. They will feel bad if they are excluded by being left outside, when the rest of the family are inside. Your dog should have a space that is his, such as a bed or a crate, but still be among the rest of the family.

If there are some parts of the house that you want off-limits, it's easy to teach him not to go there by reprimanding him any time he tries to enter (say for example, your bedroom). However, do let him join in with the family in communal areas, such as the living room, to help him become a content, balanced dog. Make sure your dog is never left alone outside on hot or cold days without shelter, as this can be potentially dangerous for him.

Give Your Dog Enough Exercise

Exercise is an important part of your dog's life. The amount of exercise he does will depend on his size and breed.

Some dogs need only a couple of walks per day, each one exceeding no more than 15 minutes. Pug, for example, can even suffer respiratory problems if they exercise too much. Other dogs, such as Spaniels or German Shepherds, need longer walks as they are naturally more energetic.

To know how much exercise to give your dog, make sure you research his breed thoroughly.

Traveling With Your Dog

One of the most important things to do before traveling with your dog is to make sure he is properly microchipped and up-to-date on all his vaccines, including rabies.

If you are traveling by car, make sure you start by teaching your dog to get used to car journeys by testing out short distances. It's always best to travel on an empty stomach, to avoid car sickness. Make sure the car is well-ventilated. Although it looks cute and adorable, don't let your dog travel with his head sticking out of the window, as this can actually cause eye injuries. Also, never leave your dog alone in a car on a hot day. This can actually be very dangerous for him!

If you are traveling with your dog by plane, make sure you call the airline beforehand, to learn their company procedure regarding traveling with pets. If you are flying internationally, check the destination country's rules, as each country has different approaches to pets entering their territory.

Key Takeaways

In this chapter, we looked at some of the basic care needs your dog requires to be healthy and happy.

- ☐ When you first get your dog, take him to the vet for a check-up.

- Your dog needs proper nutrition and regular feeding times. He also needs to feel a part of the family, have regular exercise, annual vet checks, and be groomed frequently if he has long fur.
- Make sure your dog gets enough exercise.
- Dogs are social creatures. It's okay if some parts of the house are off-limits. However, do let him join in with the family in communal areas.
- Traveling with your dog is a fun way to explore new places together, but make sure he is microchipped and vaccinated first.

FINAL WORDS

Having a dog is one of the most rewarding things you can possibly do.

Nothing beats that friendly face when you get home from work, or that unconditional love that only a dog can give. They give so much joy, which makes it our responsibility to make sure we take care of them and treat them like family!

Unfortunately, some dogs can be 'written-off' as problem pets, simply because their owners:

- underestimated how much work they are
- took a bad approach to their training, or
- picked the wrong breed for their lifestyle

As a result, so many adult dogs get left in shelters and, sadly, remain there for the rest of their lives.

Having an adult dog as opposed to a puppy can be so rewarding. You will notice that the dog will remain forever grateful that you provided him a family. I personally have always found immense satisfaction in taking care of adult dogs and the love I get in return is priceless.

I hope this book has inspired you to think about getting an adult dog, to see that they aren't that hard to train, and to realize they can be just as adorable as puppies.

Best of luck for you and your canine pal, and I hope you both have a wonderful companionship together.

BONUS CHAPTER: GETTING STARTED WITH PUPPY TRAINING

This book, *'Dog Training 101'*, was all about training an adult dog. I've made the argument that getting an adult dog can be a lot of fun and very rewarding.

But what if you still want to get a puppy? And witness how, under your guidance, that puppy turns into a well-behaving grown-up dog?

I totally understand!

Puppies are the cutest thing in the world, aren't they?

Yet they can also be little rascals...

Like children, they need to learn boundaries. They can't help showing puppy behavior. It's up to you to teach them how to be a dog.

That is why I wrote the book '**Puppy Training 101**: *The Essential Guide to Raising a Puppy With Love. Train Your Puppy and Raise the Perfect Dog Through Potty Training, Housebreaking, Crate Training and Dog Obedience.*'

Below, you will find the **first chapter** from this **bestselling book** as a <u>free bonus</u>.

It's my way of saying **thank you** for:

- reading this book, and
- taking it upon you to care for a dog.

You rock!

So, let's get started, shall we?

***

"Training a puppy is like raising a child. Every single interaction is a training opportunity."

Ian Dunbar

Key Takeaway: *Puppy training is about getting your puppy to listen to you. It is important to understand what to teach your puppy, when to teach it, and how to teach it.*

Puppy training starts as soon as you bring your puppy home. Whatever your pup does, you will need to react in a proper manner, or he will end up learning the wrong things. You must already be anticipating the joys of having a puppy, however it isn't going to be a cakewalk. Puppies are cute little bundles of joy, full of curiosity and a pleasure to be around. However, it can also get exasperating at times. If you are well equipped to respond properly to the challenges of having a new puppy in the house, then the housebreaking period for you and your pup will be shorter and stress free.

There are certain things that you should get right when you are raising a puppy. Routines help in reassuring the puppy. For instance, his bowls for food and water should always be placed in a constant place. You will need to teach your puppy:

- a daily routine
- where his food bowl is placed
- the times of the day when he will get to eat
- where his bed is, the time he needs to go to bed
- the time when he gets up

- when he goes for bathroom, and also
- when he gets to go for a walk or play

It would be a mistake to think that the manner in which these routines are taught wouldn't matter. It does matter. If you make use of the right method of teaching, then your puppy would be a well behaved on and will be happy too. If you make use of the wrong methods to teach, then your puppy will start making his own decisions and try to fit you into his life. It should be the other way around.

Teach With Words

You should teach your puppy a few words after your pup has learned the two most important words. These two words are:

- 'NO', and
- 'GOOD'

It's not just the routines that you will need to teach your pup. You will need to teach it words as well. Whenever your puppy does something that you appreciate, show your appreciation by saying "good", and if your puppy does something undesirable then say "no". You can start with this when your pup is about two months old.

These words should be taught in a proper manner. Your body language and tone make all the difference. If you get your puppy when it is more than three months old, you should start teaching these two words immediately.

Biscuit Training Should Be Avoided

Puppies love treats. However, coaxing good behavior with treats should be avoided. Don't rely on treats for training your puppy. You might be wondering what is wrong with it. When you start practicing "biscuit training", you are giving up the decision-making power to your puppy. Depending on whether or not your puppy is hungry, your puppy will decide to listen to you. This allows your puppy to believe that he doesn't have to listen to you.

This doesn't mean that you should deprive your puppy of treats altogether. Treats can be used for motivation, especially while teaching tricks. However, this should be a reward and not the method of teaching itself. Coaxing a puppy to do what you want on a daily basis will not help in training him.

Respect Training

Your puppy will pay attention to you only if he respects you. Your puppy should know that you are the leader at home. Without any respect, your puppy might learn the words and the routines, but will not listen to you. Your puppy's disrespect can be traced back to improper training. Too much of coddling will also lead to it. Your puppy should be taught who's the boss at home, if you want him to listen to you. Respect isn't something that you can get almost right. There needs to be consistency and you should keep doing it regularly.

This book, Puppy Training 101, will help you in figuring things out in this respect. A dog can learn a lot of words, and there isn't a better way to get him to understand what you want him to do and not to do, than to choose deliberately the words that you want him to learn. Knowing the words, you want to teach will be of no help, if you don't know how to teach. You don't have to expect your dog to listen to your child's stories. However, you can expect him to listen carefully to you. He should be eager to follow the directions you give him.

Let's take a look at the puppy-training schedule.

Crate Training

You can start crate training when your puppy is two to three months old. A crate will help in protecting your puppy from household accidents and it comes in handy when you want to housebreak your puppy. The crate would be your pup's sanctuary. Don't think of this as a pup's jail. If you do, then your puppy will start thinking the same too.

Initially, your puppy might not be happy to have his movements restricted. But it won't take long before he will go on his own to his crate for catching a quick nap, or to just retreat from all the household activity. For a new puppy, a crate will not only help in housebreaking, but it will also double up as a place for him to sleep in. When your puppy gets used to the crate, it gets really easy to take him to the vet or even for trips in your car.

Housebreaking

When your puppy is two to three months old, you can start with housebreaking training. A two-month old puppy is as good as an infant baby. They won't have much control over their bladder. Especially a small breed puppy. They don't develop control over their bladder for several months. Still, you should start your efforts at housebreaking since you get your puppy home.

Start out by establishing a pattern. This will help your puppy to cooperate with you as well. However, if you get this wrong, housebreaking will be nothing short of a nightmare. Most owners don't realize it until their puppy has had an accident in the house. These accidents will start becoming a routine, and it is really difficult to change this pattern. There are different ways in which you can start this out. This would include making use of a crate, a doggy door, or even a litter box for smaller breeds. You will learn more about this in 'Chapter 7: Housebreaking Your Puppy in 4 Easy Steps.'

Acceptance

You will also need to start handling your puppy. This is the only way in which he would accept everything that you do with him. Your puppy will need to see you as the leader in the home. Being the leader doesn't mean that you will simply have to keep deciding what's okay and isn't okay for your puppy. For instance, brushing, bathing, clipping your pup's nails, putting a collar on, a harness, or even giving your pup a pill. When it comes to these things, it is you and not your puppy that gets to decide what needs to be done. The best way, in which you can do this, would be to include some respect lessons along with the vocabulary lessons. If you teach the words and the puppy respects you too, then acceptance will follow suit.

Gentleness

Furthermore, you will need to teach your puppy that he needs to be gentle while interacting with others. He shouldn't nip or chew on people's hands or feet. Just like with acceptance training, being gentle should also be taught to your dog. A puppy is usually taught gentleness by his mother, when she (firmly) corrects the puppy while playing. Your job is to take over from there. You are your puppy's parent.

So, it is not just about caring, but also about correcting the puppy when he starts going wrong somewhere. You will need to teach your puppy to show restraint. You are the one who gets to set limits about good and bad behavior. Remember this.

Household Rules

You will need to teach your puppy about the behaviors that are acceptable and aren't acceptable in the house. Is he allowed to chew on shoes? No. Is he allowed to jump on someone's lap or sit on the furniture when others are present? You get to decide this, and everyone in the household should follow the same too. Is he allowed to enter the kitchen while food is being cooked? This might be unsafe for the puppy, so probably no. Even simple things like whether or not he is allowed to take socks from the laundry pile, sleeping in your bed at night, or even barking at strangers when he sees them from the window.

You will need to decide on the household rules, and then be consistent in making your puppy listen to you. If you have decided that something isn't acceptable, then convey the same to the others in the house too. You shouldn't confuse your puppy.

Tips for Older Puppies

You might think that the training schedule might be different for an older puppy. Well, it really isn't. Regardless of the age of the puppy, the training schedule should be the same. You will need to start out with vocabulary training. Start out with the basic routine, praise, corrective words, crate training, acceptance training, gentleness, and even household rules. So, if your puppy is still eating off your hand, barking at strangers, or doesn't stop when you tell him to, this would be the right time to start out with the basic training. Start out with simple and essential words like no and good, before moving onto the words like stay, sit, or even heel. Respect will always need to come first regardless of his age.

Move on to other words after he gets to understand the basic ones. Like walking on the leash without tugging at it, coming to you when called, lying down or staying still, waiting at the door even when it's open, to stop barking when you tell him to and so much more. All these skills would involve your puppy learning up new words. It is not just about learning what these words mean; it is also about doing what they mean. You will need to teach these words in a specific manner. This will help in your puppy seeing you as a leader. Giving him treats won't be of any help.

Leadership definitely doesn't mean hitting your puppy, or making use of choke collars. There are certain little things that you will need to do and say while interacting with your puppy. All puppies will misbehave from time to time. However, the manner in which you respond to them makes all the difference. If you keep responding in the wrong manner, then the puppy will keep on misbehaving. If you respond in a desirable manner, he will think of you as the leader. It is best if you can get this right since the beginning. With a new puppy, you get the chance to teach him all the right habits and correct them whenever he does something wrong.

***

This is the end of this bonus chapter.

Want to continue reading?

Then get your copy of "Puppy Training 101" at your favorite bookstore!

DID YOU LIKE THIS BOOK?

If you enjoyed this book, I would like to ask you for a favor. Would you be kind enough to share your thoughts and post a review of this book? Just a few sentences would already be really helpful.

Your voice is important for this book to reach as many people as possible.

The more reviews this book gets, the more dog lovers will be able to find it and learn how to properly train their puppy.

IF YOU DID NOT LIKE THIS BOOK, THEN PLEASE TELL ME! You can email me at **feedback@semsoli.com**, to share with me what you did not like. Perhaps I can change it.

A book does not have to be stagnant, in today's world. With feedback from readers like yourself, I can improve the book. You can impact the quality of this book, and I welcome your feedback. Help make this book better for everyone!

Thank you again for reading this book and good luck with applying everything you have learned!

I'm rooting for you…

BY THE SAME AUTHOR

NOTES